# ART AND HISTORY
# PETRA

Text by
Dominique Tarrier

*Project and editorial conception:* Casa Editrice Bonechi
*Publication Manager:* Monica Bonechi
*Picture research:* Serena de Leonardis and Sonia Gottardo
*Cover and videolayout:* Laura Settesoldi
*Text:* Dominique Tarrier
*Translation:* Eve Leckey
*Editor:* Simonetta Giorgi
*Map:* Studio Grafico Daniela Mariani, Pistoia.

© Copyright by Casa Editrice Bonechi, Firenze - Italia
Tel. +39 055 576841 - Fax +39 055 5000766
E-mail:bonechi@bonechi.it
Internet:www.bonechi.it

*Printed in Italy by* Centro Stampa Editoriale Bonechi.

*Photographs from the archives of Casa Editrice Bonechi taken by* Paolo Giambone.

*The photos on page 68 are courtesy of* Rami G. Khouri.

**ISBN 88-8029-840-2**

* * *

# HISTORICAL BACKGROUND

Of all the civilizations which inhabited the land of Jordan, the Nabataeans have left the most impressive memorials, especially in their capital city where numerous façades carved out of the rock still exercise a quite unique fascination. The history of Petra must, however, have begun much earlier than the arrival of the Nabataeans as a Neolithic settlement dating from some 7,000 years B.C. and consisting of six ascending rows of dwellings has been discovered in the area around Baidha. During the first millenium B.C. the Edomites, a people mentioned in the bible as having categorically refused to let the Jews, lead by Moses, enter their territory, settled here.

In a complete and systematic take-over of the plains on the summit of the Umm al Biyarah plateau, at a height of 1,400 metres, the Edomites made a firm stronghold of the area. The remains of numerous dwellings dating from the 7th century B.C. have been found as well as cisterns for collecting rain water. The presence of the Nabataeans is recorded only from the 4th century B.C., a new civilization whose origins are still unknown, though most probably they were part of a wave of migration from the south of the Arabian peninsula. This ethnic group progressively took control of southern Jordan and made Petra the centre of a trading network based mainly on the transport of precious materials, such as incense, myrrh and spices, towards the Mediterranean. In 312 Antigonus, who had succeeded Alexander the Great as ruler of Syria, twice attempted to conquor Petra, mounting military campaigns lead respectively by Atheneus and by his own son Demetrius Poliocretes, both of which failed completely.

On the whole, however, little historical information is available and indeed the first reference to a Nabataean king, Harith, or Aretas, dates from the third century. Although it is known that a Nabataean kingdom, independent from Seleucid rule, existed from the early 2nd century, only one king from this period, Harith I, has passed into history for having given refuge to the high priest Jason. In fact a precise chronology of the Nabatean kings based on more substantial documentation can be drawn up only from 100 B.C. onwards.

The Nabataean kingdom reached its greatest glory under Harith III Philodemus (84-56 B.C) who also weilded considerable influence over Damascus for a certain period, and especially with Harith IV (9 B.C. - 40 A.D.). Malik II (40-71) and Rabbel (71-106), his successors, succeeded in defending the Nabataean kingdom against the influence of Rome, rapidly spreading throughout the region at the time, and the economic problems caused by changes to the main trade routes. This period was also one of intense agricultural activity, traces of which can still be seen in southern Jordan and the Negev.

On the death of Rabbel II in 106, Trajan ordered the governor of Syria, Cornelius Palma, to make the Nabataean kingdom into a Roman province of Arabia with the capital in Bosra. No longer a capital city, Petra, however, was honoured with the title of metropolis, the 'mother city', and its sphere of influence does not seem to have diminished as a direct result. At the time of the Emperor Hadrian's visit in 130, the city was re-named Adriana Petra and seems to have shown no sign of decline over the next few centuries, even becoming the seat of a bishopric at the close of the Roman era, with the creation of a new province, Palestine Tertia.

During the Byzantine period the city was repeatedly hit by earthquakes, destroying many buildings which were never subsequently rebuilt; these were clearly one of the reasons for the gradual desertion of the entire area. From the 7th century on references to the city became increasingly rare, and finally ceased altogether, only making a brief resurgence during the 12th century when it was temporarily occupied by the Crusaders - who do not seem to have recognised the place, however, since they called it the 'Moyse Valley' - and again a century later when Sultan Baybars passed through. Thus Petra was no more than the name of a legendary city when, at the beginning of the 19th century, an intrepid Swiss traveller, Johann Ludwig Burckhardt, succeeded in arriving at a mysterious place where access was prohibited and which he identified as the ancient and fabulous capital of the Nabataeans. So began the series of explorations and excavations which have revealed the magnificence of this forgotten city to the entire world.

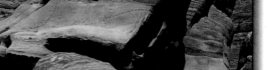

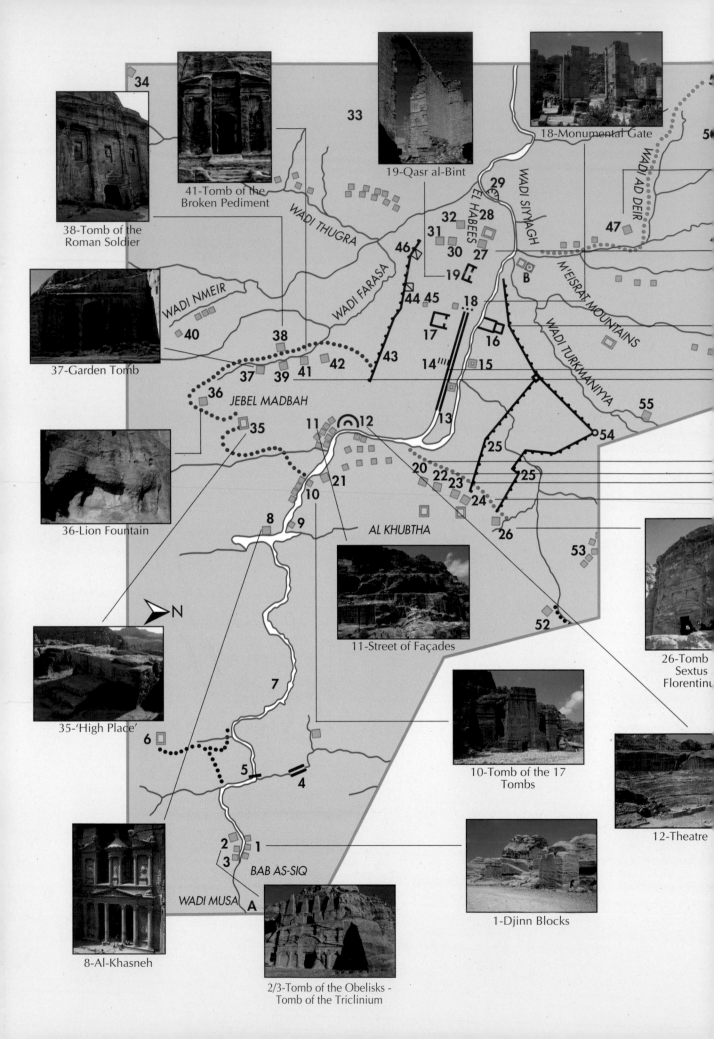

34

41-Tomb of the
Broken Pediment

38-Tomb of the
Roman Soldier

37-Garden Tomb

36-Lion Fountain

35-'High Place'

8-Al-Khasneh

33

19-Qasr al-Bint

18-Monumental Gate

WADI THUGRA

WADI NMEIR

WADI FARASA

WADI SIYYAGH

WADI AD DEIR

M'EISRAT MOUNTAINS

WADI TURKMANIYYA

EL HABEES

40

38

37    39    41    42    43

36

JEBEL MADBAH

35

11    12

46

44    45

17    16

14    15    13

18

29

32    28

31    30    27

19

B

47

55

54

25    25

20    22    23    24

26

52

53

21

10

8    9

AL KHUBTHA

N

7

6

5    4

2    1
3

BAB AS-SIQ

WADI MUSA    A

11-Street of Façades

10-Tomb of the 17
Tombs

26-Tomb
Sextus
Florentinu

12-Theatre

1-Djinn Blocks

2/3-Tomb of the Obelisks -
Tomb of the Triclinium

51-Ed-Deir

47-Lion Monument

27-Al-Habis Museum

16-Temple of the Winged Lions

14-Colonnaded Street

39-Triclinium

20-Urn Tomb

23-Corinthian Tomb

24-Palace Tomb

22-Silk Tomb

The landscape around Petra consists of a series of high plains, separated by deep faults, overlooking wide valleys, which for many centuries have provided communication routes.

# PETRA

The name **Petra is** derived from the Greek word meaning 'Rock' and perfectly evokes the rocky plateau which is the visitor's first impression as he approaches the city.

Unlike other ancient cities whose urban structure is set amidst a familiar geographical context, Petra is surrounded by sandy plains, highly susceptible to erosion and therefore deeply scarred with channels and wadis where the heavy winter rainfall runs. These plains consequently form a series of plateaus, all quite separate and each equipped with their own infrastructure, from sanctuaries to stores and cisterns which would guarantee a supply of water.

Given Petra's unusual position, it is clear why early settlers made use of the terraces half way up the sides of the slopes, or the plateaus high above the centre of the city. Moreover, it is this kind of partially built rock dwelling, found throughout the area, that has given the city the typically spread-out character which visitors often find so disconcerting. Although the wadis clearly dissect the area, they are also, paradoxically, unifying elements since they provide communication roads connecting the various parts of the city. Indeed, where wadis were wide enough, low walls could be built to make terraces and gardens which were well exploited. On the plains around the Musa wadi, which crosses the area from east to west, numerous centres of population developed, such as **Al-Baidha** in the north and **Sabrah** in the south. Periferal to the main centre, these settlements fulfilled the dual roles of agricultural production and resting places for the caravans.

Still today, as in ancient times, the main route of access is in the area of Ramlah and runs parallel to the bed of the Musa wadi. Although recently substantial alterations have been made here to accommodate increasing tourism, some of the ancient structures are still easily identifiable such as the two large tanks near to the *Forum Hotel*. Also worthy of note is the rock tomb, known as the *Khan*, to the right of the entrance, where the recent removal of various modern constructions has once more fully revealed the façade.

*The start of the visit. Horses can be hired for the first part of the route.*

*The Djinn blocks, tower tombs carved out of the rock face.*

*Many conduits converged in this area. Note the cistern cut out of the rock on the right.*

# THE DJINN BLOCKS

The first monuments on the road to Petra are three enormous rectangular blocks situated on the right side of the wadi. Now separated from the rocky mass behind them, these blocks have been given various imaginative names, though they are now generally known as the **Djinn blocks**, a term which derives from the Arab. Many theories existed concerning them and many believed they were cisterns until they were finally identified as tombs; one even still has a stepped pyramid at the top, although the upper section has been lost. Two of these tombs have a burial chamber which opens towards the east. At the corners of the third block two pilasters, linked by a quarter column, frame two recessed half columns. In 1978 a close examination of the block revealed that at the top was a channel 2 metres deep

and measuring 2.20m x 1.20m. This type of monument is found elsewhere in the settlement and is clearly related to the tower tombs so common throughout classical Arabia, such as the famous monuments at Palmyra in Syria. In this kind of structure the tomb itself forms part of a rectangular or cube-shaped commemorative monument which is, in fact, simply an enormous funerary stele. This structure is rather similar to the pyramidal *nephesh* seen throughout the city of Petra singly, in groups or sometimes near tombs. The *nephesh*, engraved or cut into the rock, represent the soul and image of the deceased whose tomb may be nearby though it is often at some distance; the stele is therefore specifically intended to record the name and memory of the dead person.

*The area at the entrance to Petra is known as Bab el Siq.*

*Although built one on top of the other, these two tombs are quite separate. The obelisks on the upper tomb represent the deceased buried within; the façade below belongs, in fact, to a triclinium.*

# THE TOMB OF THE OBELISKS
# AND THE TOMB OF THE TRICLINIUM

Architectural structures similar to those just described can be seen nearby, on the left, on the façade of the **Tomb of the Obelisks**. In fact, the four obelisks framing a small niche on the upper part of the façade are actually *nephesh* which symbolically represent the persons interred within the burial chamber, dug deep into the rock face. The tomb contains five separate chambers known as *loculi*, two of which are on each side of the entrance while the fifth is on the wall opposite. The latter tomb is that of the figure represented in the central niche on the façade which therefore has a similar function to that of the obelisks or *nephesh*. Immediately opposite the tomb, on the right side of the wadi, an inscription in Greek and Nabataean records the fact that Abdmank had a tomb for himself and his descendents built in this place. It is generally believed that such an inscription was intended for by-passers to read and must therefore refer to the Tomb of the Obelisks.

An enormous **triclinium** lies beneath this tomb yet the two are in no way related; not only has the tomb a different axis, but it is also considerably older. The façade, which dates from the second half of the first century A.D., appears slightly squashed as there was insufficient room to build it any higher. The tomb represents a synthesis of almost all the decorative elements found in the monuments of Petra. In particular there are two orders of pilasters - smaller in the upper part which includes the curved arch belonging to the upper element of the pediment above the lower section of the façade. The pediment of the upper section is, instead, split. The interior consists of a single large room with three seats cut into the rock. Its appearance is rather similar to a Roman dining room and consequently the tomb is known as the **Triclinium**. On the exterior, to the sides of the entrance, two small rooms house ten loculi resting on the bare earth. The central room, similar to many others in Petra, was used mainly for banquets which were held not only when a burial took place, but also on anniversaries and ritual celebrations.

The tunnel dug into the rock through which the waters of the Wadi Musa were deviated.

The immense height of the walls on either side gives the narrow gorge of the Siq its striking appearance.

# BAB EL SIQ

A few hundred metres further ahead, passing various structures including the remains of a system of conduits and many rooms cut into the rock, the course of the wadi twists towards the right in the direction of the **Bab el Siq**. Originally, in fact, the wadi flowed through the Siq gorge, but at the time of the Nabataeans a dam was built slightly to the north, deviating the river into a **tunnel** 88 metres long and 6 metres deep, carrying it first towards the Wadi Muzlim and then the Wadi al-Matahah, eventually emerging to follow its natural course again crossing the area in the direction of the Wadi Arabah. The existence of such a large and lengthy tunnel is clear and important evidence of the level of technical skill achieved by the Nabataeans in hydraulic engineering. It is also, however, an indication of the dimension of the floods which have always occurred in the wadi during the winter and spring rains.

The ancient dam has long since disappeared, but in order to protect the city, a new structure had to be built, though it is quite different from the original which connected the two banks. While construction work was being carried out a group of *nephesh* dating from the first century A.D. was discovered on the right of the wadi, in front of the entrance to the Siq. One of these steles, commemorating a certain Petraios who had died and was buried at Jerasa, has provided us with some useful information, indicating that the Nabateans called their capital Reqem or Reqmu, a name which could well have derived from the unmistakable variegations of Petra's sandstone.

A rock chamber in the stone wall directly in front of the Siq houses the **Triclinium of Aslah**, named for its owner. The dedication to Dushrat on the far wall here dates from the first year of the reign of Aboud I, and therefore approximately 95 B.C.

Before continuing, one may visit the area to the south east known as **al-Madras**, where many inscriptions, niches devoted to various cults and rock chambers are to be found.

*Despite its narrowness, the Siq has always been one of the principle routes of communication in the area.*

*There are numerous inscriptions and votive niches along the Siq. Of particular interest is the hemispherical god statue of Dushrat, venerated in Dera'a, above right.*

# THE SIQ

The **Siq**, leading into the centre of the city, is a natural gorge approximately 1.5 km. long and extremely narrow; while the steep cliff faces on either side often reach a height of 100 metres, the gorge is never more than 2 metres wide. An arch once stood at the entrance though today only the bases still exist.

Along the right wall of the Siq a conduit is visible, cut directly into the rock and still enclosed with slabs of rock in several places. This channel was part of the city's extensive network for carrying water drawn from the natural wells near the village now known as Wadi Musa. Along the walls are more votive steles as well as god statues, small rectangular or round bas-reliefs. These stones, which are found on their own or in neatly arranged groups along the walls of this fascinating passageway, are symbolic images of the gods venerated by the Nabataeans. The highest divinity was Dushrat, an image of whom can be seen in the Siq in the form of a hemispherical stone resting on a low base, a form typical of the city of Dera'a.

15

The Siq, as well as being an important communication route, seems also to have had a religious purpose, gradually preparing the visitor for his arrival in the heart of the city. This would explain the presence of numerous votive bas-reliefs and commemorative inscriptions engraved on the walls of the gorge. Moreover, pilgrims too regularly travelled along this road as is revealed by an inscription seen to the left of the hemispherical god statue and dated during the later half of the 2nd century A.D. This commemorates Sabinus Panegiriarcas from the city of Dera'a, described as the leader of a pilgrimage.

About halfway along the route is an isolated block carved with a niche which is flanked by pilasters crowned by Nabataean capitals. Above is a frieze with a metope and triglyphs. Inside the niche are two god statues set on a pedestal. The larger, almost one metre high, has stylized eyes and nose, features frequently used to represent the goddess Al-Uzza, who is found throughout Petra and in the sanctuary of Wadi Rum. The niche is at approximately the same height as the ancient paving which once covered the Siq. Still visible quite nearby, set into the wall on the right, are some terracotta pipes which belonged to the second system constructed to bring water into the city from the Wadi Musa.

Finally, just as the Siq seems to narrow even further, between the two increasingly overpowering walls we catch our first glimpse of Petra's most famous monument, Al-Khasneh.

*The god statues are sometimes found in groups.*

*On the right, at the bottom of this votive niche, is a god statue representing al-Uzza.*

*The fascination of the façade of al-Khasneh as it appears at the end of the Siq.*

*On the following pages: two views of al-Khasneh by David Roberts, a 19th-century Scottish traveller, one of the numerous artists who visited Petra leaving records of the most important monuments.*

# AL-KHASNEH

The name **Al-Khasneh,** meaning 'The Treasury', derives from the presence of an urn at the top of the monument which the inhabitants of the area during the 19th century claimed had contained the treasure of the Pharaoh at the time of the Exodus. Indeed, legends concerning hidden treasure were for long used as an excuse to forbid foreigners access to the area.

Considerable controversy developed regarding the monument. The earliest archaeologists, taking into consideration only the stylistic aspects of the construction and probably unwilling to believe that the Nabataeans could have been responsible for such a spectacular monument, generally maintained it was of the Roman period and more precisely the second century A.D. Later studies have, however, revealed that it is very similar to known examples of Alexandrian architecture, thus confirming that it was heavily influenced by Hellenistic models. Magnificent in the soft morning light when the rose red sandstone glows softly, Al-Khasneh was built into an immense cliff face and the surrounding steep walls protect it like a gem in its case. The harmo-

nious façade, forty metres high and 28 wide, has two orders built in a richly exuberant Corinthian style.

The lower order has an entablature with a pediment supported by four columns in the centre set slightly further forward to the recessed entrance. Engravings and old photographs (as can be seen on the following pages) show that when Petra first became the object of exploration and study, one of the columns was almost completely ruined. Careful restoration by the Department of Antiquities in 1960 re-established the former graceful symmetry of the façade. Decorating the space between the lateral columns are bas-reliefs portraying two figures on foot leading a horse, whom some have interpreted as the Dioscuri, the mythical twins Castor and Pollox, sons of Zeus and Leda.

*Beside and below left: the Dioscuri who, according to Greek mythology, accompanied the souls of the dead. Below right: Jordanian soldiers belonging to the Desert Patrol in front of the Treasury.*

In the centre of the second order of the façade is a circular structure, or *tholos* surrounded on three sides by a portico. On either side of this are pavilions, each crowned by a half pediment which enhance and emphasize the corners. Between the columns of the portico are images of Victory sculpted in relief, while those on the lateral pavilions are decorated with Amazons. Portrayed in the centre of the *tholos* is Isis with a cornucopia in one hand and a patera in another, traditional attributes of Fortune. This bas-relief has been compared to an image of Queen Bernice, wife of Ptolomy III, which can be seen on an Alexandrian vase dated 2nd century B.C.

The decorative designs on the façade also include many figures of animals, such as the eagles crowning the pediment, the sphinxes at the ends of the lower entablature as well as the facing griffins on the frieze. Other decorative elements consist of plant motifs, in particular the foliage seen on the frieze and the volutes of the capitals. These volutes are an original creation by the Nabataean sculptors and are so skilfully executed that they seem to have been inspired by the work of Alexandrian craftsmen.

In the tympanum of the pediment a "Female figure amidst foliage" is portrayed and at the summit, immediately beneath the image of Isis in the *tholos*, a solar disc is seen held between two bull's horns and ears of wheat. The presence of these elements, together with the figure of Isis dominating the central pavilion, has lead many to believe that al-Khasneh was a temple dedicated to the supreme Egyptian deity, clearly much revered in Petra as many other images of her are found throughout the city. In fact, however, all the bas-reliefs decorating the monument, from the urn on the summit to the Dioscuri who traditionally accompanied the souls of the dead on their last journey, are all quite clearly funerary symbols. Al-Khasneh was not therefore a temple but a monumental tomb and this is confirmed by the arrangement of the interior.

*The doors on either side of the vestibule are decorated with attractive sculptural work which shows the influence of Greek art.*

*Originally the internal walls were decorated with designs in stucco work.*

# THE INTERIOR OF AL-KHASNEH

Crossing the vestibule and descending a short flight of steps we enter the main room. Compared to the magnificent façade the **interior** seems strangely bare and plain. At regular intervals along the wall, however, small indents can be seen which in the past contained stucco designs of a style identical to that on the outside. Originally therefore, the interior must have had quite a different aspect. Indeed, these elegant decorations often served to soften the somewhat rough-cast effect of the walls in many of the rock dwellings and chambers, lending them an appearance more similar to that of normal buildings.

On the far wall is an alcove preceded by a few steps: this probably contained a sarcophagus. On each side of the vestibule is a door, finely decorated and surmounted by an ochulus which gave light to the rooms behind. The purpose of the larger room, almost square in design on the left, is unknown, though it may have been the chamber where funerary banquets were held. The benches cut into the rock, such as those in the Triclinium tomb, may have been replaced here by normal seats.

Although there is no longer any doubt as to the purpose of this monument, it is more difficult to establish its ownership with any certainty. Such a majestic tomb however, could only have been built for one of the greatest Nabataean rulers. Considering the stylistic characteristics of the building, one is tempted to think of Harith III Philodemos (84-56 B.C.) whose name itself indicates his admiration for the Greek civilization and culture.

# THE END OF THE SIQ - THE TOMB OF THE 17 TOMBS - THE STREET OF FACADES

Beyond the Treasury, the gorge of the Siq continues for another 200-300 metres, gradually becoming wider. The number of tombs increases in this area and on the whole their façades fall into two recognizable categories. The first is that known as **Hegra**, and is characterized mainly by the presence of a door, exactly the same as those seen on the façades of Greek sanctuaries, with a double entablature and crenellations crowning the upper element. Several rather important burial chambers belong to this group, including in particular the **Tomb of the 17 Tombs**, lying at the far end of the right wall, which contains numerous pyramid-shaped sculpted *nephesh*.

Along the **Street of Façades**, are tombs built on four levels, resembling towers with one or two rows of crenellation at the top. These reflect an oriental style of architecture and belong to a much older historical period.

*The gorge of the Siq widens towards the end until it reaches the Street of Façades (below right).*

*Petra's Theatre, dating from the beginning of the 1st century A.D., was built on the right of the main roadway.*

*A view of part of the stage showing one of the side entrances.*

*Petra's Theatre in a drawing by David Roberts.*

*On the following pages: the auditorium is set over 18 metres deep into the rock face.*

# THE THEATRE

Immediately beyond the Street of Façades are the 33 tiers of the **Theatre** which could seat some 5,000 people. The steps, cut out of a particularly crumbly pale reddish-grey sandstone, have always been heavily subject to erosion by rain water flowing down from the surrounding plains. The tiers are arranged in a semi-circle around the stage which measures fifty metres at the widest point.

*Small flights of steps lead to the tiers of seats.*

*Erosion has severely damaged the theatre steps.*

*The façades of numerous tombs were destroyed when the amphitheatre was built here.*

Access was via several lateral passageways on both sides of the stage and at a later date some small stairs were also built providing access directly to the upper part of the auditorium. In order to build the theatre, the rocky wall behind was deeply excavated causing the loss of many façades and burial chambers in this area. Today all that remains to remind us of ancient splendour, are some empty hollows, somehow inevitably recalling huge cinema projection rooms.

At the back of the stage were the scenic constructions and the lateral entrances, the upper part of which were surmounted by vaults.

*Access to the tiers of seats was through grandiose side entrances, such as that seen on the left in the photo.*

*The scenic backdrop, partially restored.*

These entrances and vaults still remain standing, while only the foundations of the scenic backdrop now exist as, when the ancient dam fell into ruin, the water from the wadi flooded and severely damaged the entire area. Although restoration work has recently been carried out, this was specifically limited to straightening and reconstructing some of the columns and clearly falls short of recreating the original appearance.

For practical reasons the Theatre must have been set back from the road which passed in front. Also at this junction, supported by a low wall, was one of the branches of the city's water system. For a long time the Theatre, like the Treasury, was considered to date from the Roman period, but the various excavations which have been carried out lead to a revision of this date, and it is now believed to have been built in the first century A.D.

Although undoubtedly the most important, given its size and location, this is not the only building of its kind in Petra. Another theatre, entirely built of stone as opposed to carved out of the rock, has been discovered in the outlying area of **Sabrah**, 6 km. further to the south. This settlement, which also has several impressive buildings, was an important mining and caravan centre.

# THE SILK TOMB AND THE CORINTHIAN TOMB

Continuing towards the north is a small tomb, not particularly original in its decorative style, consisting of four inset columns and a crenellated cornice. Its fame and the name of the '**Silk Tomb**' is, in fact, due to the magnificent veining of the façade, which glows with delicate and harmonious colours ranging from white to bright pink, tinged with shades of blue, pink, orange and grey.

Nearby is the second of the monumental tombs, known as the **Corinthian Tomb**. The façade, exposed to the effects of wind and sand, has unfortunately suffered badly from erosion, to such an extent that in places the relief sculpting has completely disappeared. Despite its advanced state of deterioration, arriving from the Siq one is immediately struck by the similarity between this tomb and al-Khasneh, although it is not so lofty in form and the two orders of which it is composed are not particularly harmonious. The upper order, consisting of a short portico surrounding a *tholos*, seems to be copied directly from the Treasury, although it differs from it as it contains no sculptural figure and is therefore a purely architectural element. The lower order, which is similar to that of the Triclinium tomb at the en-

*This monument is famous for the coloured streaks on the façade, rather than for its decoration.*

*The overall appearance is unbalanced: the lower part is too wide compared to the upper level.*

trance to Petra, rests on a podium and has eight inset columns with capitals decorated with plant volutes. The overall appearance is even more impressive due to the miniature pilasters and pediment which form a base to the upper order. The façade has five doors; the largest and the one on the right provide access to the main room where numerous alcoves have been cut into the walls on the right and opposite. The doors between the columns to the left open onto further small, square-shaped rooms which most probably were also burial chambers. The style of the tomb, a forerunner to 2nd century baroque, enables us to date it to a period prior to annexation by Trajan. Given the layout and the size of the structure, it was most certainly a royal or princely sepulchre.

# THE TOMB OF SEXTUS FLORENTINUS

The remains of the Byzantine walls can still be seen near to this tomb, slightly set back in relation to the Nabataean bastion crossing the Wadi al Matahah, between the heights of al-Khubthah and al-Masara. Here a large *birkeh* was constructed which, after running along the north side of the al-Khubthah massif, ended at one of the branches of the system for supplying water from the Ramlah cistern.

A little further north, on the tip of a rocky spur, is the last important monument along the western wall. The façade is framed by a pair of pilasters crowned with Nabataean capitals which support the entablature. Above is a pediment with a rounded arch in the centre of which is a bas-relief portrait of a "Female figure amidst foliage". Above the arch rises an eagle while the triangular pediment crowning the façade is surmounted by an urn. The Latin inscription above the door, engraved on the lower lintel, describes the monument as **the tomb of the governor of the Province of Arabia, Sextus Florentinus.** The complete dedication is as follows: "To Titus Aninius, son of Lucius, of the Gens Papiria, Sextus Florentinus, Triumvir charged with the coining of gold and silver, Military Tribune of the 1st Legion (Minerva), Quaestor of the Province of Achaia, Tribune of the Plebs, Legate of the 9th Legion (Hispania), Proconsul of the Province of Narbonensis in Gaul, Legate of the Emperor Augustus, Propraetor of the Province of Arabia, beloved father, according to his last will and testament".

Various documents show that Sextus Florentinus could only have been governor between 126 and 130, and one papyrus shows him as certainly holding this office in the year 127. The inscription is therefore of particular interest for two reasons: on the one hand it provides valuable information for establishing the date of the tomb; on the other it shows that Sixtus Florentinus explicitly requested to be buried in Petra and that the place chosen for his tomb, which is fairly similar to other Nabataean sepulchres, was located quite near to the

*A Roman Governor is buried in this Nabataean tomb which is similar in design to many others.*

Royal Tombs. This was, in fact, a somewhat unusual initiative and is indicative of the fascination that the beauty and magnificence of the place exerted over a high-ranking Roman official.

Continuing and returning along the Wadi al Matahah, we come to the **House of Dorotheos,** situated on the right side and consisting of two triclinia cut from the rock face. The one on the left has the same name written on it twice, leaving us in no doubt whatsoever concerning its ownership.

The Colonnaded Street along the west wall of the al-Habis massif.

The centre of the city was crossed by a road long before a paved street with columns was made.

# THE COLONNADED STREET

For safety, as well as for practical reasons, the Nabataeans preferred to inhabit the higher plains of Petra. However, from the beginning of the 1st century B.C., a plan of urban re-organization was progressively carried out, involving, in particular, the basin of the Wadi Musa whose course had already been deviated and checked. The existence of a complex system for drawing water from the springs around the edges of the settlement in order to supply the centre of the city is clear evidence that the organization of the entire area had been planned in considerable detail.

This part of the city was organized along an axis which ran parallel to the right side of the wadi, creating what is now usually known as the **Colonnaded Street.** In and around this street the remains of the most important monuments are to be found; with one or two exceptions, most of the area has now almost completely returned to desert due to the dreadful earthquakes which occurred during the

first millenium and in 551 in particular, which severely affected the area and caused the destruction of many of the buildings. Catastrophies of this kind were, moreover, one of the main reasons for the decline and eventual desertion of the city.

At least part of the paving in the colonnaded street has been preserved and probably dates from the Roman period, since there are no signs of any form of paving earlier than this. The street, six metres wide with some of the columns appropriately reconstructed along the left side, may be best seen from the **Nymphaeum**, on the right hand side. This monumental fountain was dedicated to river and spring deities, the Nymphs.

Shops and houses were built along both sides of the *cardo* during the Byzantine period. Fragile constructions such as these, and the lower part of steps leading to temples and other buildings were unable to withstand the earthquakes, however, and only the foundations remain to be seen.

On the right side of the wadi, near to the Nymphaeum, recent excavation work has been concentrated on an ancient **church** and has revealed a magnificent mosaic pavement decorated with natural motifs in the transepts, including personifications of the *Four Seasons*, the *Ocean*, the *Earth* and *Wisdom*. The church dates from the 5th century and, as in most buildings of the Byzantine period, considerable use was made of material taken from much older constructions. Some papyri have also been discovered here and are now being carefully studied and restored.

*The eastern side of the al-Khubthah massif seen from the Colonnaded Street.*

*Another view showing the western side of the street.*

*Some of the columns have been reconstructed demonstrating the origin of its name.*

Monumental steps on the left of the road lead up to the South Temple.

The Monumental Gate seen from the Colonnaded Street.

The Monumental Gate seen from the tèmenos of Qasr al-Bint.

# THE SOUTH TEMPLE

At the far end of the colonnaded street, on the left, are the remains of a **monumental staircase** - the 'propylaeum steps' - which lead to a first courtyard, followed by a large terrace where a great temple, now being excavated, once stood. The outline of this Nabataean temple, built at a height of 28 metres and now known as the **South Temple**, had already been uncovered at the beginning of this century. It was preceded by a flight of stairs leading to the pronaos, 8 metres deep and flanked by four columns. The entrance had imposing columns on either side, and the interior, measuring 28 metres in length and 18 wide, had 22 columns placed around three sides. The plan of the temple, dating from the 1st century, has not yet been completely deciphered, but it would seem that the structure had many features in common with the other sanctuaries in Petra, already described.

# THE MONUMENTAL GATE

At the end of the street is a majestic **triumphal arch** which, with the Qasr al-Bint, is one of the best preserved stone structures in Petra. This three-arched gateway lead into the tèmenos, the sacred area of Petra's most important temple. It was built during the 2nd century and is therefore later than the *cardo* itself which, in fact, probably had to be widened and the paving partially removed in order to build the foundations of the gate. Originally the arch was framed by two tower-shaped structures and was built on a raised stone platform made of blocks taken from various buildings. The façade on the side of the *cardo* has four free-standing columns and capitals decorated with animal and plant motifs. The architectural structure of the internal façade consists of two doorways with pairs of quarter columns and two partially recessed columns in the centre. The central gateway has capitals with plant volutes while the others are clearly Nabataean in style. The gateway is decorated with small stucco panels representing figures of deities, geometric designs and various Hellenistic style elements.

*Unlike the drawings by David Roberts in the previous pages, here we have only a hazy impression of the monument portrayed.*

54

*It is clear from the fractured column in the foreground that they were unable to withstand the frequent earthquakes.*

*The Temple of the Winged Lions.*

# THE TEMPLE OF THE WINGED LIONS

Opposite the monumental gate, on the right side of the wadi, is another temple known as the **Temple of the Winged Lions** for the capitals carved with these animals. A bridge, the remains of which are still visible across the Wadi Musa, leads from the paved street to an initial rectangular terrace. There was probably a second courtyard in front of the sanctuary, partly supported by vaults. The east and west walls of the cell or naos were decorated with five semi-columns, corresponding to the ten columns of the portico. In the centre was a platform surrounded by a colonnade and accessible from two lateral stairways. The image of the god to whom the temple was dedicated would have been inside this structure; most probably this was al-Uzza, the goddess with stylized human features represented on the god statue discovered in the north portico. The layout of this sanctuary is very similar to that of other Nabataean temples, especially one at **Khirbat al Dharih**, in southern Jordan. A block of marble discovered in the crypt bears an inscription recording donations of gold and silver engraved with a date which corresponds to 27-28 A.D. Nearby were the workshops of sculptors and painters who worked on the decoration of the temple, including the architectural stucco work much of which was later housed in the interior. Between the columns were stuccoed niches and it is interesting to note that some of the fragments of painted decoration are very similar to the later Pompeian style.

Along the western side of the temple are traces of the line of ramparts which ran north along the Wadi Turkmaniyeh, ending in a round tower, known as the **Conway Tower**, built to reinforce the Nabataean city walls.

Opposite the tower, on the other side of the wadi, is the **Turkmaniyeh Tomb** noted for the magnificent inscription on the façade, unique of its kind in Petra and one of the most beautiful examples of Nabataean writing to be found in its original location. The text describes the group of buildings which constituted the funerary complex and places it under the protection of Dushrat and of all gods.

*Remains of the vaulted structures which supported part of the sanctuary.*

*The platform inside the main sanctuary.*

*The colonnade around the interior of the sanctuary.*

Qasr al-Bint seen from al-Habis.

Qasr al-Bint seen from the Temple of the Winged Lions.

A view of the entrance showing the north wall and the portico.

A detail of the arch leading into the sanctuary.

# QASR AL-BINT

Beyond the **Monumental Gate** is a large paved courtyard 180 metres long, which formed the tèmenos of the **great temple.** On the south side the courtyard is flanked by tiers of seats and at the far end, lying on the same axis as the **temple,** is a monumental altar raised on a podium and reaching a height of 23 metres. Built of sandstone blocks with the addition of wooden fetters, it is almost an exact square measuring approximately 28 metres on each side. A flight of 22 steps of white marble lead to a recessed portico, also of white marble, with four columns; this in turn opens into the main chamber of the temple, in the opposite wall of which are three openings. The central one, surmounted by an arch and decorated by inset semi-columns, was the *adyton* where a god statue was housed. This most probably represented the god Dushrat, the supreme divinity who, considering the etymology of his name - 'He of Seir' probably derived from the Seir mountain range which rises opposite the temple and dominates the entire northern area. The building on the east side was probably used for ritual banquets

*The west side of al-Habis. The museum is in the centre of the photo.*

*The museum has numerous sculptures and the showcases contain many items of all kinds found during excavations in Petra.*

attended by the entire assembly of priests entitled to officiate at the temple.

An inscription discovered on the south wall of the tèmenos definitively dates the temple as late 1st century B.C.

Both the internal and the external walls were covered with plaster and paradoxically the external decoration has better resisted the effects of time and wear, while on the inside all that remains are the small holes where the facing was fixed. On the east façade the relief stucco work forms a frieze of pilasters further decorated with bas-relief panels. The south side has a similar series of pilasters, but here there is also a small building with six columns, surmounted by an entablature and crowned by an arched pediment flanked by two half pediments.

To the west of the tèmenos is the rugged outline of the al-Habis massif, which can be reached by climbing a rocky stairway partially rebuilt to meet the requirements of modern tourism. These stairs linked the numerous rock chambers dug into the cliff face, and in particular the many dwellings, one of which is now the museum.

# THE AL-HABIS MUSEUM

Displayed on the terrace in front of the **museum** and in the room inside are numerous sculptural and architectural fragments as well as blocks of stone engraved with Greek and Latin inscriptions providing much information, discovered in various excavations in Petra, in particular at the tèmenos. Arranged in the showcases are collections of ceramics, jewellery, statuettes and fragments of painted stucco work. It is worth mentioning that the Bedouins, who settled in Petra at the beginning of this century, make reproductions of variable quality of some of these items for sale to tourists. There have recently been various initiatives to encourage the Bedouins, who live in rock dwellings, to leave Petra and move out to neighbouring areas.

The Nabataean scuplture of Petra is noticeably different from that of other Nabataean settlements and has a quite original local style which clearly reflects an oriental influence, especially evident in the facial expressions which are treated with particular attention. In Petra sculpted figures were generally classical in style and mainly copied Greek and Roman examples. The numerous representations of gods or mythological figures housed in the museum quite clearly demonstrate this, as do the bas-reliefs portraying *Aphrodite*, *Athena* and *Dionysus*. Other sculptures seem to be of foreign origin, however, such as the statue of *Heracles* found in excavations at the Theatre and now dominating the entrance to the Museum.

*Blocks of sculpture housed in the museum.*

*Many Bedouins come here to sell souvenirs to the visitors.*

# THE NEW MUSEUM

A second **museum** has recently been created on the north side of the Wadi Musa, beside the **Rest House**. One of the most fascinating sculptures exhibited here is the god statue found in the north portico of the **Temple of the Winged Lions**. An inscription on the pedestal indicates that this is the goddess *Hayyan bin Nabbat*. The form of this title, which does not state the precise name of the goddess represented, is common to many of the dedications; the divinity is not named directly but is only referred to with a place name or even the name of the royal family or occasionally a single feature or detail. In fact, according to ancient Semitic tradition, the Nabataean gods, unlike Greek and Roman gods, were ony ever identified by epithets which described actual attributes. It has already been mentioned that Dushrat means "He of Seir" and even the two supreme goddesses of the Nabataean pantheon are commonly referred to as al-Uzza and Allat, meaning respectively "She who is most powerful" and "The goddess". The god statue from the Temple of the Winged Lions, which is rather similar to the one already described in the Siq, in fact presents in fact the typically anthropomorphic image of al-Uzza. It has very clear stylistic similarities to a series of bas-reliefs found in **Hajjar bin Humeid** in southern Yemen, and in **Taymā** in central Arabia and can be identified as a quite autonomous Arabian style, in contrast to Petra's Hellenistic art.

The sculpted stone blocks are a category on their own. These include friezes such as that on page 66, originally consisting of a pair of winged lions, the one on the right now sadly lost, framing a similarly winged Eros.

*The New Museum seen from the al-Habis massif.*

*The interior of the New Museum.*

64

*A god statue representing al-Uzza with the characteristic stylized features.*

*A sculpture in the Greek style.*

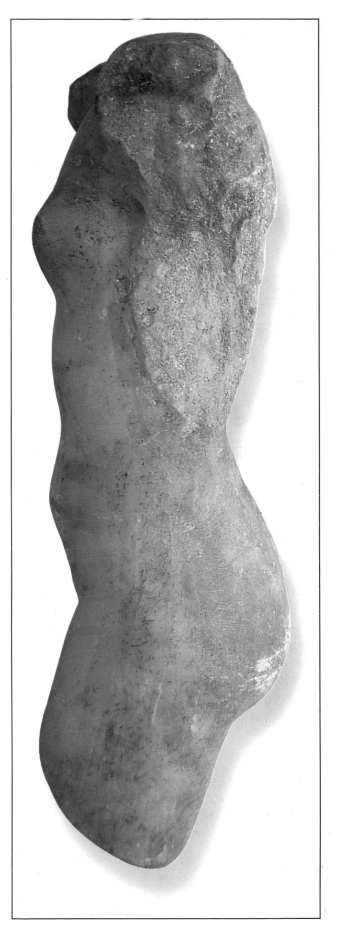

The capitals on Nabataean monuments have many original features, quite unlike Vitruvius' models. The Nabataean capital is, in fact, a rather simplified version of the Corinthian capital and resembles a slightly rough-cast block, the curving corners of which look not unlike horns with a small leaf occasionally applied to the base, and a central fleuron which is no more than a slight protruberance. Other capitals may be defined as the raceme or foliage type and, with their extremely varied designs, are one of the most original aspects of art in Petra. These capitals derived from the plant motif decorations on friezes and cornices around doors and were first transposed to the flat surface of pilaster capitals and then subsequently to the capitals of columns.

*A bas-relief portraying a winged Eros, originally flanked by two similarly-winged lions, though the one on the right has been lost.*

*Corinthian capital decorated with foliage.*

*A capital with a Medusa's head on four sides.*

An example of the latter is reproduced on page 67: the acanthus leaves or vine fronds are framed on either side by two curving corner elements which end in a volute. This basic decoration is enriched by various plant motifs, such as flowers or bunches of grapes, or even animals such as the winged lions which replaced the volutes on the capitals of the temple named for them. This is the most frequent style to be found though there are also examples of capitals where the plant motifs are replaced by mythological subjects. On the four sides of the capital seen below on page 67, for example, is a head of the Medusa.

Before leaving the museum it is worth taking a look at the ceramics on display. In fact, Nabataean pottery is famous for both the painted and undecorated items which are indisputable evidence of a highly refined technique and are considered some of the most important and interesting creations left to us by this civilization. The pottery consists mainly of bowls, cups and chalices, notable for their incredible egg-shell fineness and colour which ranges from pale pink to red. According to their shadings and decoration, the items of pottery are classified into two, chronologically successive, styles.

The first seems to have come into being at the beginning of the 1st century B.C. and to this group belong the pink or orange bowls with decorations painted in bright red, consisting mainly of a motif of palmettes in a halo design, clearly of Greek derivation. The second, much more common than the earlier style, developed during the early Christian period and was popular throughout the following century. The technique remained unchanged but the surface became a deeper red, while the decoration is a much darker, even dull, shade. The decorative motifs are more varied but also more stylized, and include palmettes, pomegranates, pairs of cones, peacock eyes and jagged leaves. Many other kinds of pottery were made in addition to this 'luxury' standard of product. The most frequently-found items consist without doubt of extremely fine crockery with delicate ribbing, the most common examples being ointment jars and jugs.

*The purpose of this room, which looks not unlike a dovecot, is still a mystery. Beside: the Pharaoh's Column.*

## THE COLUMBARIUM AND THE PHARAOH'S COLUMN

On top of the al-Habis massif (which means literally 'the prison') are the ruins of a Crusader fortress, while scattered over the slopes are numerous sites all now identifiable as funerary, cult or domestic structures. Quite easy to reach on the west side there is also a "High Place". Only one of these sites has, until today, remained a mystery despite various theories proposed concerning its purpose: the **Columbarium** is a room dug out of the rock with rows of narrow niches etched into the side and far walls, giving it the appearance of a dovecote. One theory suggested that the niches were intended to house funerary urns but, apart from the fact that this was not a common practice in the Nabataean area, they are also too shallow to have been practical receptacles at all.

On the right is the **Unfinished Tomb**, one of the best examples of the technique used by the Nabataeans to create façades in the rock face.

Less than 300 metres away, opposite the Columbarium, is a **column,** the matching pair of which lies collapsed on the ground beside. Immediately surrounding these are the remains of various buildings and it is quite probable that these columns once framed the entrance to one of these.

## THE ROAD TO ED DEIR

*Starting from Qasr al-Bint, we reach the road to **Ed Deir** (51) by crossing the bed of the Wadi Musa, leaving the al-Habis massif on the left. Following the valley in a northerly direction for a few minutes we reach the first flight of steps leading up to the plateau where the summit of the Deir massif lies. Following the itinerary shown alongside, it will take an hour to reach the top. The excursion is more enjoyable in the afternoon as the path is in the shade and the façade of Ed Deir can be seen bathed in a golden light. If, on the other hand, you prefer a magnificent view over the Wadi Arabah to the west, it is better to set out in the morning.*

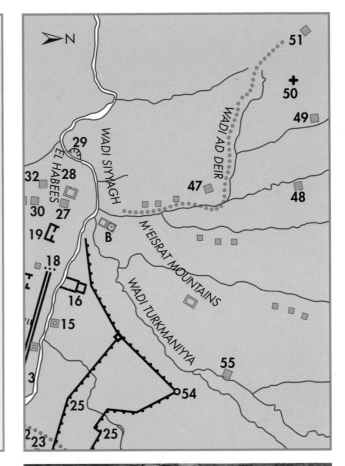

The façade of the Triclinium of the Lions.

# THE LION MONUMENT

Ten minutes walk brings us to a narrow valley which leads to the **Lion Monument** (in fact a triclinium) named after the animals sculpted in relief which frame the doorway. The façade is very similar to that of many others and this lead in the past to some confusion concerning the purpose of the monument. The doorway originally had a window above and due to continual erosion these now resemble a large keyhole. The façade is framed by pairs of quarter columns, which have Nabataean-style capitals with extremely simplified plant volutes. Above is a frieze decorated with triglyphs and metopes, the ends of which are decorated with heads of the Medusa. In the tympanum of the triangular pediment, surmounted by an urn which crowns the entire structure, is a decoration of leaves and fronds. The internal chamber has three seats, now almost completely buried under sand, and a small niche in the far wall. The style of the façade dates this triclinium to the mid 1st century A.D.

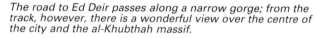
*The road to Ed Deir passes along a narrow gorge; from the track, however, there is a wonderful view over the centre of the city and the al-Khubthah massif.*

*On pages 72-73: a view of Ed Deir and the rocky spur on which it is built.*

# THE ROAD TO ED DEIR

Shortly after the Triclinium, the road passes through a narrow opening, beneath some scree which almost closes the path. After another fifteen minutes walk the path divides, leading towards Ed Deir on the left. Taking instead the road to the right we reach the **Tomb of the Three Urns**, which is, in fact, a biclinium. The façade is decorated with pilasters and pairs of quarter columns with Nabataean-style capitals, and an entablature crowned by a triangular pediment with an urn positioned at each point. Inside two seats face each other, while the third is now barely discernable. To the right at the back of the room, a tomb, probably of a much later date, has been dug in the ground close to the wall. The structure itself is dated mid 1st century A.D., the same period as the **Tomb of the Lions**.

Returning to the main road, after a further forty minutes, we reach a gorge lying to the right of an area generally known as **al-Hamman**. The area, also known as **Qattar ad-Deir**, has a triclinium and groups of votive niches and god statues, one shaped like a cross with a double crosspiece, as well as cisterns fed by water from a small rivulet which flows out of the rock.

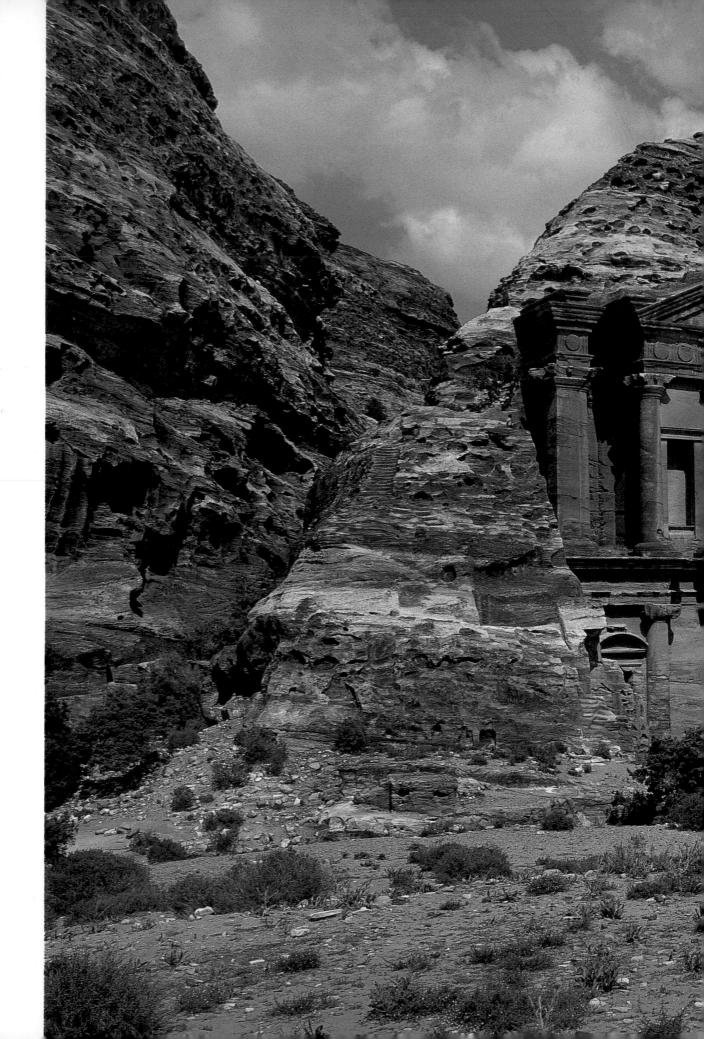

Ed Deir in a drawing by David Roberts.

*The monumental façade of Ed Deir is almost 40 metres high.*

# ED DEIR

Continuing along the same road, we pass many rock chambers, some of which still bear inscriptions engraved by Christian hermits. The road finally opens out onto a large terrace on the east side of which is the monumental building of **Ed Deir**. The name, meaning 'the monastery', recalls the monks who lived here in ancient times, though a group still inhabited **Jabal Harun** at the beginning of the 13th century. The presence of Christians in this area is also recorded elsewhere, such as in the name *Mughur an-Nasara*, meaning the 'Caves of the Christians'. The enormous façade, cut into a cliff face of yellow sandstone, is 47 metres in width and almost 40 metres high; similar in style and structure to al-Khasneh it is, however, slightly less graceful but still extremely restrained. The lower part has eight columns with Ionic style capitals, framing a central doorway, slightly recessed, while between the columns on both sides are empty niches with arched pediments above.

The upper part has a *tholos* decorated with a frieze of triglyphs and metopes and flanked on either side by pavilions, also surmounted by identical friezes and with half pediments. As on the lower order,

these three elements contain empty, rectangular niches. Two pilasters and side walls enclose the entire upper order. The *tholos* is crowned by a huge urn, 9 metres in height, which can be reached by a narrow flight of steps on the left of the tomb. Apart from the frieze, capitals and pediments, the entire structure is without additional decoration and this somehow endows the monument, which dates from the time of Rabbel II, with a certain majesty. Along the side walls of the internal chamber are low seats which enclose an alcove, confirming the hypothesis that the banquets of the cult of Aboud I were held in this room. Aboud defeated the Seleucids in 85 B.C. and was divinified, becoming the object of a specific cult, evidence of which can be seen in numerous inscriptions. One such inscription, found near to Ed Deir, commemorates the followers of the cult who gathered in honour of the god Aboud. Such brotherhoods, which were quite common in eastern cultures, formed under various names and titles in order to preserve the memory of their members and were quite numerous in Petra. Many of the triclinia seen here were connected to such institutions.

# ROUTE TO THE 'HIGH PLACE'

*Alongside is the route leading up to the* ***'High Place'*** *(35). The sequence is in reverse order with respect to the signposts but followed in this direction the route is not only much more pleasant but also less strenuous for the visitor. It is therefore useful to take as a point of reference the Pharoah's Column, to the north of which lies the area of al-Katuteh. The path then turns to the east and on reaching the southern walls of the city leads towards the entrance to the gorge of the Wadi al Farasa. The trip along this trail, avoiding the heat of the day, takes about three hours at a normal pace.*

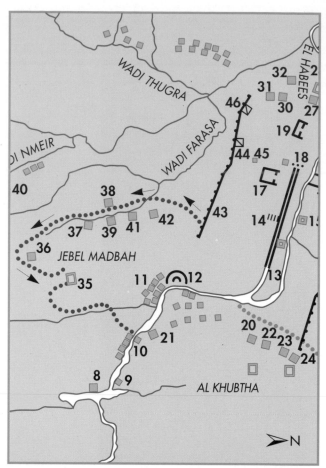

*These tombs with oriental style façades are at the entrance to the gorge of the Wadi al-Farasa.*

# THE RENAISSANCE TOMB

Along the left side near the entrance to the wadi is a series of tombs surmounted by merlons, oriental in style and similar to those at the end of the Siq. Continuing along the gorge, the first tomb is usually referred to as the **Renaissance Tomb**. The elegant façade consists of a door with an arch above, supported by pilasters. On either side are two tall, inset columns and pilasters which support a double entablature and pediment. On the same side, at a distance of some fifty metres, a second tomb is built into a recess which is slightly raised above the level of the path.

The Tomb of the Broken Pediment.

# THE TOMB OF THE BROKEN PEDIMENT -
# THE TOMB OF THE ROMAN SOLDIER - THE TRICLINIUM

The façade of the **Tomb of the Broken Pediment** has two lofty columns on either side of the entrance which support double entablatures and half pediments. The interior of the tomb was never finished as, of the six loculi planned, only four were ever made. In front of the tomb is a wide terrace where several basins were dug, one of which is octagonal in shape. Continuing along the gorge, we arrive at an area probably once surrounded by a wall and laid out as a garden, with three colonnaded porticos enclosing a tomb and triclinium. The sepulchre, known as the **Tomb of the Roman Soldier** or the **Tomb of Statues**, has a central doorway surmounted by a frieze with triglyphs and metopes and

crowned by a triangular pediment. The façade itself is decorated with four semi-columns supporting the entablature and pediment which is also triangular in form. Between the columns are three niches, framed by pilasters and entablature, each containing a statue. The central figure is portrayed wearing a short tunic beneath a form of armour, with a cape on top, while the figures on either side are of young men, also wearing capes. These could well represent the owner of the tomb with his two sons and if this were so the sculptures would in fact represent a form of *nephesh* as is the case with several other monuments. The interior of the tomb consists of two chambers, the larger of which contained numerous vaulted alcoves. Facing this tomb is the largest **triclinium** in Petra. Three doors, each with a window above, provide access to the building which, despite lacking a decorated façade, is one of the lovliest of the rock chambers in the area. The coloured streaks of the walls which today so fascinate the visitor, were originally entirely covered with a plaster decoration, reproducing a classical design consisting of grooved columns set into the walls and surmounted by capitals and cornices. Along the side walls were five false windows while on the far wall five niches imitated doors, corresponding to the three entrances which alternated on the inside with two window-niches, thus creating an overall sense of symmetry. The seats are unusual not only for their size, but also because they are separated from the walls by a passage behind them.

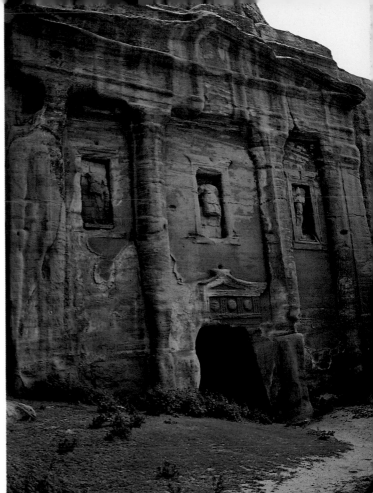

*The tomb is named for the statue in the centre of the façade which is thought to represent a Roman soldier.*

*The Triclinium.*

*The Garden Tomb.*

# THE GARDEN TOMB - THE LION FOUNTAIN

About 100 metres past this structure and slightly higher up, is the façade of the **Garden Tomb**, a very simple burial place, opening directly from the outside and with only two columns on the façade, flanked by pilasters which support the entablature. A second room, further inside, constituted the burial chamber. There is a small terrace in front of the tomb, reached by a low flight of steps. Originally this part probably had a roof and was enclosed by stone-built walls. A room, about nine metres wide, can be seen higher up on the terrace; although this is now open to the sky it must once have had an arched roof matching the arches seen on the opposite wall. The walls are decorated with twelve niches in imitation of windows, similar in style to the triclinium described above. On the south side the room was enclosed by a stone-built wall of which nothing is now left. Although the building does not have any seats, it too must have been a triclinium, the purpose of which is still unknown. Cut out of the rock in front of the room is a most impressive cistern, 28 metres long by six wide.

The structure had stone walls which accentuated its height. The tank was filled by water from one of the branches of the complex water system supplied from the Brak spring three kilometres further to the south. This cistern served the entire area and its considerable size is evidence of how populous it had become. Another branch of the same hydraulic system fed the **Lion Fountain**, located quite nearby on a vast rock face at the end of a small valley which was once closed by a dam. This monumental fountain, in the form of a lion, is some 4.5 metres long; water, carried along a small conduit which passed above the head of the lion, poured from its mouth.

*Erosion has worn away all the detail leaving only the outline of the lion sculpted on this monumental fountain.*

Standing at the centre of the 'High Place' is a repository where god statues were housed.

The 'High Place' seen from the north: the altar is seen on the far right.

The 'High Place' seen from the south; note in particular the triclinium.

# THE HIGH PLACE

Higher up are numerous interesting graffiti and commemorative inscriptions as well as a god statue surmounted by a medallion, representing Dushrat in the guise of Dionysus. Continuing we reach the **High Place**, the entrance to which is indicated by two obelisks. These heights provide an excellent viewpoint from where we can enjoy a splendid view over the massifs of **Umm al-Biyarah** and **Jabal Harun**. From here we can also make out a large area consisting of levelled ground about 64 metres in length within which lies a rectangular zone measuring 14.5 metres by 6.5. This represents a triclinium which seated all those entitled to attend the banquet held after ritual ceremonies.

On the west side instead, is a large square block known as a *motab* in Nabataean, a term meaning 'repository' or 'throne'; preceded by three steps, this structure was a collection point for the god statues carried in processions. On the left side is a circular shaped altar reached by another flight of three steps at the side. The presence of a small channel where blood was collected to anoint the sacred stones, is clear evidence that the altar was used for sacrifice. Two basins dug out of the rock nearby held water for cleansing and purifying. In the centre, immediately in front of the 'repository' is a small platform intended for the priest who was officiating, as in biblical descriptions. Although it is not as old, the High Place is of a similar tradition of those in Cana, mentioned in the Old Testament where, however, only scattered remains in a very poor state of repair are now to be found. Petra's High Place is, on the other hand, perfectly preserved and its structure enables us to identify the influence of Arab religions particularly with regard to the concept of the holy area, forbidden to profane use, as well as the ritual of the procession of the god statues which could have taken place in the passageways winding around the repository.

*A general view of the 'High Place' with the obelisks.*

*This obelisk, 6 metres high, represents one of the most important Nabatean gods, perhaps Dushrat or al-Uzza.*

It is not known precisely what kind of sacrifices were celebrated in these High Places, but on the way down ramps are visible in several places, suggesting that animals such as sheep, goats and even camels were used. At the end of the ceremony, a 'meal of communion' took place to which all those present were invited. As well as this quite exceptional sanctuary, other structures of the same kind are to be found on the heights surrounding the city centre. These 'High Places' must, in fact, have been the first sanctuaries created by the Nabataeans when they settled here and it is therefore obvious that each group wished to establish its own place of cult worship. Moreover, it is quite probable that the design of some temples, such as that of the Winged Lions, is the result of modifications made to a primitive sanctuary in order to adapt it to the classical style of architecture.

Although no direct reference is ever made to the gods venerated in the High Place, the two blocks shaped like **obelisks** nearby provide some evidence for speculation. These blocks, six metres high and thirty metres apart, were made by carving away the rock surrounding them. Thus the obelisks form a matching pair of god statues which may be identified as the most important deities of the area, already mentioned, Dushrat and al-Uzza to whom the massif of Jabal al-Madhbah was probably consecrated.

Slightly further ahead, the ruins of what was once a **fortress** are visible, the towers lending it a particularly impressive appearance. It is generally believed to be Nabataean, though it is also thought to have been a Crusader castle.

Before returning along the other pathway which leads to the north side of the theatre, it is worth pausing to admire the magnificent view across the slopes of the al-Khubthah massif.

The Tomb of Uneishu can be seen in the centre of the photo.

The 'High Place' is an excellent point from which to view the lofty plains surrounding the site (seen here is al-Khubthah).

# THE TOMB OF UNEISHU

This massif, which rises opposite the Theatre, contains many **tombs built on two levels**. The most important, located on the upper level, is that of **Uneishu**, a minister of queen Shaquilat II who reigned from 70 to 75 A.D. In front of the tomb is a Doric style square, 15 metres wide and 12 deep, with a triclinium situated on the north side. The façade of the tomb, which falls into the Hegra category, consists of a door with a few steps leading up to it, decorated with a double frame including pilasters with pairs of quarter columns which support the entablature and pediment above. The burial chamber has 11 loculi and three more loculi have been dug out of the wall behind the triclinium. Originally these sepulchres were sealed by a slab of stone with the name of the deceased engraved on it. However, the area was subject to looting and we have consequently lost much valuable information.

Only two fragments have been found: one has a damaged inscription though the words "queen of Nabataea" are still legible, 'queen' here meaning 'princess', while the other provides us with the name and title of the owner of the tomb. The triclinium is a quite unique feature here, as the Tomb of Uneishu is the only one in this area, including the royal tombs, to be arranged in this manner. The door, to the left of which is a large, rectangular basin, has a window 2.5 metres high above. The seats are reached by a flight of three steps on either side. There was room for up to twenty guests, all in the lying position commonly adopted at Greek and Roman banquets. It should be noted, however, that this kind of banquet is actually of oriental origin and the influence of Greek customs was merely supplementary to practices which were already known.

The colours of Petra's rock inspired some memorable poetry by early visitors to the area. Geologists have now found an explanation for the formation of this sandstone, the oldest layers of which date from the Cambrian period and which, on first sight seem to be of a uniform dark red colour. The sandstone is streaked with light veining and when the sun lights up the façades and the walls, it is easy to see why Petra is referred to as the 'rose red city'. The characteristic streaks are caused by the presence of metallic oxides and gave rise to the Semitic name of the city, Reqmu, meaning a brightly coloured fabric.

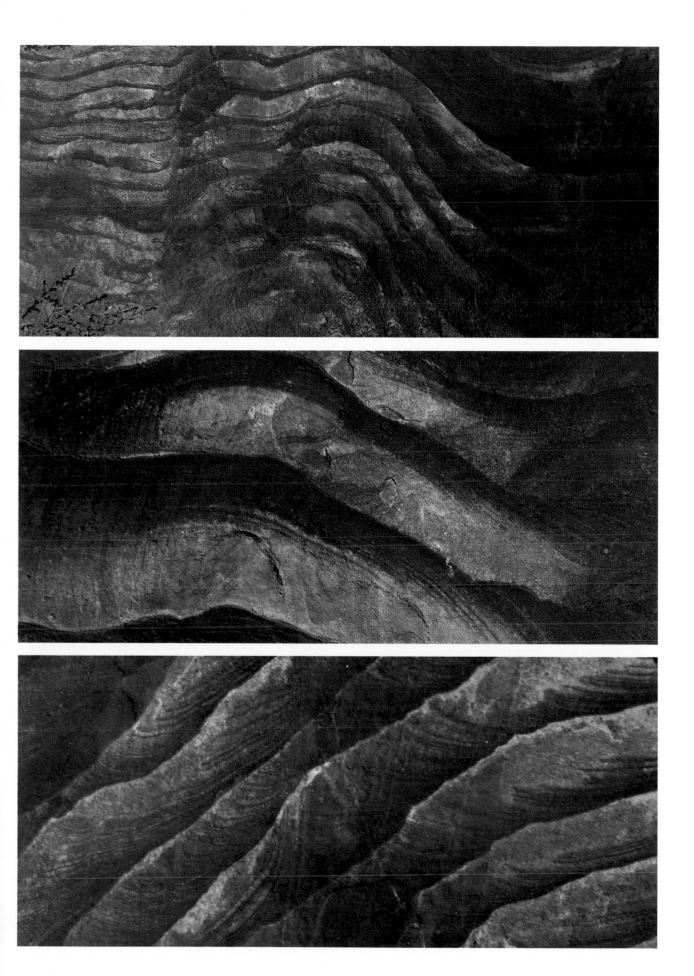

*The area around Little Petra (As-Siq al Barid) is still inhabited and many agricultural settlements are found here.*

# LITTLE PETRA
## (AS-SIQ AL-BARID)

Taking the old road which leads towards the right at the entrance to Petra, following a route much frequented since the most ancient of times, we reach an area to the north of the city. The road passes by numerous rock settlements, in particular the **Crusader fortress of al-Wu'eira,** and leads to the area of **Baidha** or **Al-Baidha**, a northern suburb of Petra which was both a stopping place for caravans and centre of agricultural production as can be seen from the presence of many stone presses and mills. Here, moreover, one of the most important neolithic settlements was discovered, dating from the 7th millenium and inhabited for over five hundred years. The Ammarins now live here, a Bedouin tribe who have given their name to the monumental cistern dug into the cliff face.

The **Al-Barid** gorge is like a
miniature reproduction of the Siq
and leads to a small sandy valley
with a myriad of rock chambers
and cisterns around the sides.
These storage tanks were fed by
rain water collected by dams
built across the wadis higher up,
a method frequently used
throughout the area. On the left,
at the entrance to the valley, is a
chamber flanked by two columns,
which probably formed part of a
dwelling with rooms on a lower
level as well. Still on the left, further ahead, is a triclinium with an
entrance 3.5 metres high, framed
by pilasters with capitals above.

*Opposite As-Siq al-Barid is a tomb
with a façade similar to that of a
temple.*

*Although the façade is not unlike that
of a temple or tomb, this structure was
in fact a residence.*

*The gorge of al Barid has many rock
chambers in the form of triclinia.*

*Erosion has created odd shapes and
forms in rocks throughout the area.*

Two triclinia can be seen in the wall on the right, with a separate room situated between them. The structure of these is no different to many of those already described, though the triclinium on the left has a series of holes on the exterior which probably housed the supports for the vaulted roof of a stonework structure. On the walls of the central room are the remains of painted plaster imitating a smooth wall covering of trimmed stone, while the ceiling seems to have been decorated with a corona design. The most famous monument of As-Siq al-Barid lies hidden at the end of the valley. A large rock chamber with two seats (a **biclinium**) is reached from some steps up the right side. The wall at the back of the chamber has a vaulted alcove with one of the rarest examples of painting still surviving in Petra. The decoration, recognizable as the late Pompeian style and rather similar to that in the House of Livia in Rome, consists of plant motifs (leaves and fronds), animals (birds) and mythological figures such as Eros and Pan.

One is tempted to imagine therefore, that some of Petra's aristocratic families preferred As-Siq al-Barid for their home, or possibly as their summer residence, due to the delightful cool air enjoyed here throughout the summer months.

*Still visible in the walls of As-Siq al-Barid are the cisterns which collected the rain water carried by a network of conduits.*

*A view of the exterior of the painted biclinium.*

# INDEX OF PLACE NAMES

# CONTENTS